Copenhagen

Kiel

Hamburg

Warsaw

uisberg

Essen

Dortmund

Kass

sseldorf

Cologne

Leipzig

Koblenz   Schweinfurt

Frankfurt

Dresden

Prague

Mannheim   Nuremberg

Karlsruhe

Stuttgart   Regensburg

Munich

Bern

Milan

Key

● Bomber Command Group Bases

✿ Bomber Command Targets

✳ Luftwaffe Targets

Series 117

This is a Ladybird Expert book, one of a series of titles for an adult readership. Written by some of the leading lights and outstanding communicators in their fields and published by one of the most trusted and well-loved names in books, the Ladybird Expert series provides clear, accessible and authoritative introductions, informed by expert opinion, to key subjects drawn from science, history and culture.

The Publisher would like to thank the following for the illustrative references for this book:
pages 17 and 19: courtesy of IWM collection (CH 13020) and (CH 12283); page 21:
Major-General Spatz's head – David E. Scherman/The LIFE Picture Collection via Getty Images;
page 43: Don Salvotore image – Public Domain (digital reproduction or scan of US Govt photo),
John Godfrey and James Goodson – original image reference courtesy of IWM collection.

Every effort has been made to ensure images are correctly attributed, however if any omission or error
has been made please notify the Publisher for correction in future editions.

MICHAEL JOSEPH

UK | USA | Canada | Ireland | Australia
India | New Zealand | South Africa

Michael Joseph is part of the Penguin Random House group of companies
whose addresses can be found at global.penguinrandomhouse.com

Penguin
Random House
UK

First published 2020

001

Text copyright © James Holland, 2020

All images copyright © Ladybird Books Ltd, 2020

The moral right of the author has been asserted

Printed in Italy by L.E.G.O. S.p.A.

A CIP catalogue record for this book is available from the British Library

ISBN: 978–0–718–18653–1

www.greenpenguin.co.uk

MIX
Paper from
responsible sources
FSC® C018179
www.fsc.org

Penguin Random House is committed to a
sustainable future for our business, our readers
and our planet. This book is made from Forest
Stewardship Council® certified paper.

The Bomber War

James Holland

with illustrations by
Keith Burns

Ladybird Books Ltd, London

On the night of 14 November 1940, Coventry, an industrial cathedral city in the British Midlands, was hit by a large raid of German bombers – some 450, led by Kampfgeschwader (Bomber Group) 100 equipped with a navigation aid called *X-Gerät*. This used pulse radio technology to create beams that could be converged on a particular target. British intelligence had managed to crack an earlier German navigation aid, *Knickebein*, but not the new technology of *X-Gerät*, which meant the Luftwaffe's bombers reached their target accurately and without much interference.

The conditions for bombing were perfect: there was enough moonlight, not much cloud and a breeze in the air. Attacking in two waves and dropping a mixture of high-explosive heavy bombs and numerous much smaller incendiaries to set off fires, the gap between the waves was timed to perfection, with the second fanning the flames of the first. In all, 503 tons of bombs were dropped, including 139 1,000kg mines – the biggest the Germans had at the time – and 881 canisters of incendiary bombs.

The target had been Coventry's motor factories, but the centre was devastated. The beautiful cathedral and medieval heart of the city were destroyed as fires raged. It was the worst single attack so far in the Blitz – the bombing of Britain's cities that had begun two months earlier on Saturday, 7 September – and was a psychological and physical blow that deeply shocked both the wider public and Britain's war leaders. In all, 18,261 British civilians were killed by German bombing from the start of the Blitz on 7 September to the end of November 1940.

Coventry would not be forgotten – neither the method of the attack nor its effects.

When Germany invaded Poland on 1 September 1939, so starting what was to become the Second World War, they did so with the Luftwaffe flying above them and supporting the army's operations on the ground. Much had been written about the role of air power throughout the 1920s and 30s, but in truth no one was quite sure how it would manifest itself in the next war, despite its use in recent conflicts such as the civil war in Spain.

Air power and aeroplane technology were changing fast and, twenty years on from the last world war, machines were very different. However, it was a safe bet that air power would play a vital role and, clearly, whichever side controlled air space would have a crucial advantage.

In Britain, air power had been at the heart of rearmament from the mid-1930s. The Royal Air Force was reorganized into different commands: Training Command, Coastal, Bomber and Fighter. Each was to operate independently as what was known as a 'strategic' air force. Bomber Command would bomb enemy targets; Coastal would help protect Britain's waters; Fighter Command would defend Britain's skies and was to be supported by the world's first – and at the time only – fully coordinated air defence system combining radar, observers, ground controllers and radio.

In Germany, the Luftwaffe had taken a different approach. Aircraft, whether bombers, fighters or reconnaissance, were grouped together into air corps and then air fleets. Their role was entirely to support the army on the ground, or as what is termed 'tactical' air power. Briefly, the Luftwaffe's Chief of Staff, General Walther Wever, planned to create an independent heavy bomber force, but when he was killed in a flying accident in 1936, his ideas died with him.

So it was that the Luftwaffe began the war with lots of fighter aircraft, Stuka dive-bombers and twin-engine 'medium' bombers, but no strategic bomber force. To begin with, this appeared to have been a good decision. As the army pressed forward, ahead of them Messerschmitt fighters shot down weak and out-of-date Polish aircraft, or bombers destroyed them on the ground. Screaming Stukas terrified soldiers and civilians alike, while the medium bombers pummelled the capital, Warsaw. No one doubted the role air power had played in Germany's rapid victory in Poland.

The Luftwaffe was again the German spearhead in subsequent attacks on Scandinavia, then France and the Low Countries in 1940. On 14 May, just four days after the Germans launched their attack on the West, the Luftwaffe's bombers struck Rotterdam in Holland, with devastating results. Fifty-seven Heinkel 111s dropped bombs on the city centre, destroying 2.8 square miles of Rotterdam's heart and killing some 850 people. Chaos ensued. The frightfulness of war and the Armageddon brought by massed bomber formations, repeatedly forecast throughout the 1930s, suddenly appeared to be a reality. The attack on Rotterdam certainly hurried the Dutch decision to surrender.

The shortcomings of the Luftwaffe's structure were, however, laid bare during the Battle of Britain that followed. After the French armistice on 22 June 1940, Germany tried to bludgeon Britain into suing for peace through the use of air power alone. Attacks on Channel shipping in July were followed by more concentrated attacks on airfields, the British aircraft industry and other communications. For the first time, however, the Luftwaffe was operating on its own, strategically, and not in the supporting tactical role for which it had been designed.

The Luftwaffe's attempts to destroy the RAF did not go very well. They had never come up against a proper air defence system before and no longer had troops on the ground supporting them with follow-up actions. Their Stukas were being decimated now they were operating in skies where they no longer had complete control, while their medium bombers – mostly Dornier 17s and Heinkel 111s – could carry only about 2 tons of bombs. Nor were there enough of them. Only one airfield out of 138 used by the RAF was put out of action for longer than 48 hours. All the while, the strength of RAF Fighter Command was growing, not diminishing.

What's more, the bombers of Bomber Command were taking the attack to the enemy. The first raid on Germany had taken place on the night of 16/17 May 1940, while, whenever weather permitted, British bombers from Bomber and Coastal Commands were attacking German landing barges building up in the Channel ports as well as new Luftwaffe airfields near the French, Belgian and Dutch coast.

Then, on the night of 23/24 August, Bomber Command struck Berlin. The raid was not very successful in terms of damage, but was followed by three more attacks on the capital of the Third Reich. Incensed, and frustrated by the Luftwaffe's failure to subdue the RAF, Adolf Hitler, the German Führer, ordered reprisal strikes on London. The first deliberate attacks on the British capital arrived on Saturday, 7 September 1940 and would continue until the middle of May the following year.

The aim was no longer to destroy the RAF but to cause as much damage as possible and to break the morale of the British people. The 'Blitz', as it became known, had begun.

RAF Bomber Command Wellington and Hampden bombers on their way to Berlin.

Although air-raid shelters had been built in readiness for such an assault and personal air-raid shelter kits issued, there were public shelters for only around half Britain's urban population. Civilian casualties quickly mounted. There were 6,968 deaths and 9,488 serious casualties in September 1940, 6,313 and 7,949 in October and 5,004 and 6,247 in November, including the raid on Coventry.

Despite this carnage, Britain's factories continued to grow in number and productivity and there was no sign whatsoever of any collapse in morale. Britain's scientists were swiftly developing counter-measures against the Luftwaffe's night-time navigation aids in what became known as the Battle of the Beams. Soon after the counter-measure to *Knickebein*, one was also found for *X-Gerät*.

Nor was Bomber Command sitting still. The night after Coventry, over 100 RAF bombers attacked Hamburg and Dutch airfields used by the Luftwaffe. The Hamburg raid caused a number of fires and heavy damage to the Blohm & Voss shipyard, and was the most successful RAF bomber raid of the war to that date.

None the less, the Luftwaffe's largely night-time bomber assault of Britain continued. From airfields near the Channel, German aircrews did not always need *X-Gerät* to locate large cities such as London or ports like Southampton, Portsmouth and Liverpool. In February 1941, Hitler ordered his bombers to focus on Britain's ports. Between 19 February and the second week of May, there were sixty-one attacks of more than fifty bombers, of which forty-six were directed against ports. Liverpool was particularly badly hit. Some 316 bombers struck Merseyside on the night of 12 March, for example, and over 500 people were killed.

A Heinkel 111 bomber over Liverpool.

Despite the relentlessness and horrific damage caused by the Blitz, only 18,000 tons of bombs were dropped on London, a figure that would be dwarfed by what was to follow in the war. In mid-May 1941, with the Germans poised to launch their assault on the Soviet Union, the Blitz abruptly ended. It had fallen a long way short of achieving its aims and had cost the Luftwaffe dear. Britain was still in the war with its armaments production on the increase, while the Luftwaffe had more than 2,000 fewer aircraft with which to support the biggest military operation ever undertaken. Fears of aerial Armageddon had been largely unfounded after all.

The Luftwaffe would continue to use air power to try to subdue its enemies, but elsewhere it was just as unsuccessful. The tiny British island of Malta, for example, was not defeated despite in the spring of 1942 briefly becoming the most bombed place on earth. Depleted as it was by the middle of 1941, the Luftwaffe's bomber force also failed to play a significant role in the war against the Soviet Union. So much had been fruitlessly wasted on Britain.

The shortcomings of the Luftwaffe as a strategic air force had been matched, however, by those of Bomber Command, which had also discovered it had neither the numbers nor its bombers the capacity to deliver the kind of ordnance that would hurt Germany significantly. Nor did it have the navigational tools for the job. British bombers had far further to travel and navigate to reach German targets within the Reich than those of the Luftwaffe along the Channel coast had to reach Britain. At night, often with cloud cover and with only basic calculations – 'dead reckoning' – to help contend with variable wind speeds, Britain's bombers proved woefully inaccurate.

In August 1941, the Butt Report was published, an independent investigation into the accuracy of Bomber Command's bombing effort. Devastatingly, it revealed that only one in three bombers had been managing to drop its bombs within 5 miles of the target. It was a huge blow for Bomber Command and there were many who questioned the ongoing bombing strategy, which was, after all, using up a considerable amount of effort and resources, not to mention young men's lives. Although they were attacking at night because it was safer, bombing remained perilous.

There was to be no change of heart, however. Air Chief Marshal Sir Charles Portal, the Chief of the Air Staff, continued to believe strategic bombing would dramatically shorten the war and save the lives of many British servicemen. More importantly, the Prime Minister, Winston Churchill, was equally convinced air power was the key to ultimate victory. In any case, by mid-1941, British factories were producing more aircraft than any other country in the world. It was too late to change tack.

The answer was to improve the means of bombing. New, bigger aircraft were on their way. Some of the finest minds in Britain were dedicated to pushing the country's aviation industry to new levels of sophistication and technological advancement – incredible new navigation aids were in the pipeline and a superb new bombsight, the Mk XIV, known as the Blackett Sight, would start trialling in early 1942.

It was bad news for German civilians, but collateral damage was not something that weighed too heavily on the minds of many of Britain's war chiefs at the time – not with parts of London and other cities in ruins and nearly 40,000 dead thanks to the Luftwaffe.

British bomb-aimer using the Blackett Sight.

There was also new leadership. One man who had watched the Blitz with bitter interest was Air Marshal Arthur Harris. Standing on the roof of the Air Ministry in London, watching the fires raging over London, he had vowed, 'They will reap what they sow.' In February 1942, he became the new commander-in-chief of RAF Bomber Command. Like his boss, Sir Charles Portal, he was an avowed believer in the power of the bomber and in bringing Nazi Germany to its knees by pulverizing its cities and industrial infrastructure.

He also recognized that a major period of rebuilding was essential before Bomber Command could deliver the weight of force required to make strategic impact. Strategic bombing would have to be conducted on a far larger scale altogether. He needed lots more bombers, four-engine heavies, not twin-engine types, and especially the new Lancaster that was just coming into service. These would demand more airfields, and with concrete runways that could operate in all conditions. He needed much better navigation tools as well. None of this could happen overnight. Harris reckoned it would take a year at least until he was ready to launch his all-out strategic air campaign against Germany.

Even so, Bomber Command was not to stand idle. In April 1942, he launched a rare low-level daylight raid using twelve of his new Lancasters against the MAN diesel plant in Augsburg. In terms of damage caused it was highly successful, but the attacking force was decimated: only five returned safely. It underlined why night-time attacks had to continue.

Bomber Harris.

Far greater success was achieved with the 'Thousand Bomber Raids'. Harris launched the first at the end of May 1942. On paper, Bomber Command only had some 400 bombers, but by scouring the Operational Training Units and other commands, and by using a number of largely obsolete aircraft, they managed to reach the magic number of 1,000 bombers. The first target was Cologne in west Germany, and the damage caused was considerable.

It also profoundly shocked Reichsmarschall Hermann Göring, the commander of the Luftwaffe, and the rest of the Nazi leadership. Two more such raids followed and, although it was too risky and stretched resources too tightly to repeat them regularly, they achieved their aim: Bomber Command was given a huge boost and their success did much to convince the sceptics that large-scale strategic bombing had a vital part to play in the ongoing war.

Also arriving by the summer of 1942 were the commanders and first units of the United States Eighth Air Force, who were to operate alongside Bomber Command. The plan was to build up some sixteen heavy bombardment groups, each with 32 heavy bombers, and three pursuit – or fighter – groups of 75–80 fighters, as well as medium and light bomber groups.

They were commanded by Major-General Carl 'Tooey' Spaatz, another committed bomber man, although he was convinced that daylight 'precision' bombing was the way forward. A hugely experienced and intelligent commander, he had been an observer in England during the Battle of Britain and the Blitz. Nothing he had witnessed had dissuaded him from this firmly entrenched stance. 'The Germans can't bomb at night,' he observed. 'Hell, I don't think they're very good in daylight.'

General 'Tooey' Spaatz.

Like Harris, Spaatz believed what was needed was ever-larger heavy bomber forces. The US had developed heavily armed B-17 Flying Fortresses and B-24 Liberators, but, because of the limitation of navigation aids, Spaatz was convinced accuracy could be achieved only in daylight. This would make the bomber force more vulnerable, but by flying his bombers in a tight defensive formation and equipping each one with thirteen .50-calibre machine guns, he believed heavy casualties could be avoided.

Spaatz had little chance to test his theories, as most of the Eighth's raids were short-range across the Channel, then most of his forces transferred to the Mediterranean after the joint Anglo-US invasion of north-west Africa in November 1942. Meanwhile, Harris continued sending his slowly growing bomber force to strike targets in Germany as well as the U-boat pens along the French Atlantic coast.

Not until the beginning of March 1943, however, and armed with a new directive from the Anglo-US Joint Chiefs of Staff to smash the German 'military, industrial and economic system', was Harris ready to launch his all-out attack. By then he had new navigation aids such as GEE, Oboe and now H2S, effectively the world's first ground-mapping radar. Marking targets was now in the hands of a special Pathfinder Force – or PFF – which flew ahead of the main bomber stream, armed with Oboe and H2S and using marker flares, helping ensure far greater accuracy when the bombs began dropping.

'I was at last able to undertake with real hope of success,' noted Harris, '. . . the task of destroying the main cities of the Ruhr.'

An RAF Mosquito of the Pathfinder Force drops flares over a target.

The Ruhr was the industrial heartland of the Third Reich and Harris's offensive began on the night of Friday, 5 March 1943 with an attack on Essen. He now had some 700 bombers, of which more than 400 were four-engine heavies. What's more, it was a number that was, at last, significantly on the rise.

Some 442 bombers were used on Essen, dropping a mixture of incendiaries and 4,000 lbs – 2 tons – of high explosives. Despite cloud cover, Essen was devastated: 160 acres of destruction, with 53 separate buildings within the Krupp armaments factory hit, 3,018 houses flattened and a further 2,166 seriously damaged. At least 482 civilians were killed – more than on any single raid to date. A major new phase of the air war had begun.

While the Battle of the Ruhr was launched, Bomber Command was also preparing a one-off strike against Germany's mighty dams. The Möhne and Eder Dams were Germany's largest and were immense feats of engineering, providing water both for civilian use and for vital industrial processes. The Möhne and the Sorpe, another large dam, supplied the Ruhr, the Eder the city of Kassel. It was hoped that, if destroyed, their loss would be calamitous for Nazi Germany.

The dams were protected by vertical anti-torpedo nets, so the challenge was to get enough explosive over those nets and against the dam walls. This, however, had been considered impossible until Barnes Wallis, an engineer and assistant chief designer at Vickers Aviation, created a depth charge that could skip across water. The idea was that the bomb would 'bounce' over the nets, hit the dam wall, sink and then, at a certain depth, explode. The explosive power would be increased by the water pressure above – enough to smash the dams.

Barnes Wallis, and trialling his invention.

Harris had been against the plan, believing it a gross waste of resources on something that appeared too fantastical to have any chance of success. His bombers were used to flying at 18,000 feet or higher and not in formation. This would require a small force of Lancasters, specially adapted to carry the 4-ton bouncing bomb – codenamed UPKEEP – to fly in formation at just 100 feet to stay below German radar detection, at night, over unfamiliar enemy territory and then drop the UPKEEP at a very precise spot dead centre of the dam and from an equally precise distance away. It seemed impossible. Even so, Portal, Harris's superior, gave Operation CHASTISE the green light.

A new squadron, 617, was formed, under the command of Wing Commander Guy Gibson, who was one of Harris's most determined young leaders. By March 1943, Gibson had flown seventy-two bomber missions, more than the fifty expected for two tours, and, notwithstanding his 'press on' reputation, was mentally and physically exhausted. None the less, he accepted the task and, despite less than ten weeks' training, on the night of 16 May 1943 he led nineteen Lancasters to attack the dams.

Gibson himself flew seven times up and down the defended Möhne Dam, drawing off enemy fire. The fourth bomb, dropped by Henry 'Dinghy' Young's crew, caused the fatal crack, so that by the time of the fifth run the dam had begun to crumble. Gibson then led the next assault on the Eder Dam, which, despite its location amongst steep hills, was also miraculously hit and destroyed. The Sorpe was badly damaged. Although eight crews were lost, the Dams Raid had been an incredible success.

Gibson's leadership during the Dams Raid was of the highest calibre and his Victoria Cross more than deserved. Huge tsunamis from the smashed dams caused apocalyptic damage, while the costs of repairing the dams and other infrastructure, at a time when the war was dramatically turning against Germany, were immense.

Bomber Command continued to hammer the Ruhr, but worse was to come for Germany. Operation GOMORRAH, an attack on Germany's second city and biggest port, Hamburg, was launched on the night of 27 July. Conditions were perfect and the British dropped millions of strips of tinfoil – known as 'Window' – to jam the German radar system.

Over three nights, some 3,500 aircraft smashed the city. The results were truly terrible. Some 42,600 German civilians were killed – more than had been killed in Britain during the entire Blitz. A further 37,000 were wounded and the old Hanseatic city was all but destroyed as a colossal firestorm developed – so big, so hellish, that the flames rose to nearly 1,500 feet. Around 6,200 acres out of 8,382 – around 80 per cent of the city – had been destroyed.

The Nazi leadership was shocked and appalled. 'A wave of terror radiated from the suffering city,' noted General Adolf Galland, the legendary Luftwaffe fighter commander, 'and spread through Germany.' The world had never before witnessed man-made destruction on such a catastrophic scale.

Harris's aim was to bring about the end of the war without the need for vast armies and the risk of losing a generation of young men, as had happened in 1914–18. He now planned ever heavier attacks, and next on his main target list was the capital of the Third Reich itself: Berlin.

By this time, the US Eighth Air Force was also building up its strength in Britain. General Spaatz was now commanding strategic air forces in the Mediterranean and Lieutenant-General Ira Eaker had taken over the Eighth. Eaker, like Spaatz, was a firm advocate of precision daylight bombing and had persuaded the Anglo-US Combined Chiefs of Staff that the Eighth should continue in this vein rather than join the RAF in night attacks as the British had been urging. He also argued convincingly that the priority bombing target should be the German aircraft industry. If the Luftwaffe could be destroyed, then strategic bombing would be easier as there was no question that enemy aircraft posed a far greater threat to Allied bombers than anti-aircraft guns.

Furthermore, the Allies planned to make a cross-Channel invasion of France in May 1944 and for that they needed air superiority over much of north-west Europe. Harris continued to believe massed night-time area bombing was the best way to win the war, but Eaker's plans were formally adopted as Operation POINTBLANK on 10 June 1943.

The trouble was, most of the Luftwaffe's assembly and components plants were inside the Reich, and beyond the range of Allied fighter escorts. Until mid-August 1943, the Eighth had not attempted any missions deep into Germany and casualties had been comparatively light.

That changed on 17 August, when 376 American bombers attacked the ball-bearing plant at Schweinfurt, some 100 miles east of Frankfurt, and the oil refinery and Messerschmitt plant at Regensburg in south-east Germany. It was a terrible day for the Eighth: some 60 bombers, or 19 per cent of the attacking force, were shot down and destroyed, more than 550 aircrew lost, and a further 11 bombers had to be scrapped and 164 were damaged.

Focke Wulf FW 190s attack America B-27 Flying Fortreses.

The bombing results against Schweinfurt and Regensburg had not justified the enormous effort and cost. Eaker realized he would have to send his boys back, but not until early October 1943 was the Eighth ready to have another crack at enemy targets beyond fighter range.

These new attempts were also very costly, culminating in a second attack on Schweinfurt on Thursday, 14 October. It became known as 'Black Thursday', as a further sixty bombers were shot down and 594 men lost. In fact, in seven days of missions into Germany, the Eighth had lost 148 heavy bombers. Despite the number of planes and men coming from across the Atlantic, that was not sustainable.

Nor was Harris's Battle of Berlin the success he had anticipated. If Hamburg had prompted any thought of a rapid end to the war through strategic bombing alone, this had quickly proved to be a false hope. This was because the Luftwaffe had been shocked into overhauling its air defence system. German night-bomber pilots were put into night-fighter planes – Me109s and Focke-Wulf 190s, known as the *Wilde Sau* (Wild Boars) – while increased numbers of two-engine night-fighters began attacking the British bomber stream en masse, equipped with improved radar and upward-tilting 30mm cannons called *Schrägemusik* to attack the unprotected belly of the Lancasters and Halifaxes. These were supported by superior early-warning systems and ground controllers. In ten raids on the capital of the Reich, Harris lost 239 aircraft – some 25 per cent of his force.

The Allied commanders were in crisis. The clock was ticking towards OVERLORD, the Allied invasion of France, air superiority was still a long way off, and the effects of bombing were falling some way short of expectation.

Focke Wulfs of the *Wilde Sau* night-fighters in action.

There was a crisis amongst the bomber crews too. Heavy losses were keenly felt on bomber bases in which crews were often housed together in hastily built Nissan huts. To return from a mission and find a row of empty beds where earlier there had been friends was hard to take. Everyone knew the odds of completing a 25-mission tour, in the case of the Americans, or a first 30-mission tour, in the case of Bomber Command, were not good. To many, it seemed impossible.

The weather didn't help. The winter of 1943 was particularly cold and bleak. Bill Byers, a Canadian pilot who had joined up with his identical twin brother, George, used to take his crew up on a test flight during the day just to get above the cloud and see some sunshine. George had been lost on his third mission; they had been inseparable all their lives until that night of 3 November.

Bomber crews rarely flew two days – or nights – in a row, and in between could visit pubs, local cinemas and generally do what they liked, although options were limited. RAF bomber crews would be told in the morning they would be flying that night. The target would be revealed during the briefing a couple of hours before take-off. They would be given supper, then they would collect their flying gear and head to their aircraft. Just taking off in quick succession, in the dark or thick cloud, was dangerous enough. American bombers flew in formation but RAF crews flew in a 'stream' – that is, out of formation. At heights of 18,000 feet or more the temperature fell below minus 40 degrees. Danger was constant: from collision, from anti-aircraft fire – 'flak' – or, most deadly of all, from night-fighters. Flying bombers was brutal.

Life was much better for the Allied fighter pilots. US and RAF pilots were reaching their squadrons far better trained than their German equivalents. All had at least 350 hours in their logbooks; German pilots were lucky if they had 100. Allied airmen were then rapidly able to improve further thanks to excess numbers of pilots per squadron, plentiful supplies of fuel and a core of combat-experienced men to teach the new boys the ropes. Their aircraft and tactics were also superior to those of the Luftwaffe.

The ingredient missing was a long-range fighter that could escort US heavy bombers deep into Germany, but by the late summer of 1943 the solution had been found. Back in May 1940, the British had commissioned North American Aviation, a small company in California, to produce a new fighter. The result was the P-51 Mustang. Despite a sleek, streamlined design and incredible manoeuvrability, the Allison engine was underpowered and the new fighter was a disappointment.

Then, in October 1942, the Rolls-Royce test pilot Ron Harker suggested putting in a new Merlin 60 engine and the Mustang was totally transformed. At 20,000 feet it could fly at 430 m.p.h., and at 35,000 feet a staggering 455 m.p.h. – 70 m.p.h. more than the Luftwaffe's fighters.

The position of the radiator also helped produce jet thrust and incredible fuel efficiency. The Merlin engine, which could be built under licence in the US by Packard, had transformed the Mustang into a superb fighter. Then, in the summer of 1943, an extra fuel tank was placed behind the cockpit. With two further auxiliary drop tanks added to each wing, it was discovered it could fly a stunning 1,474 miles. That took it to beyond Berlin and back. And that was a game-changer.

A P-51 Mustang in flight.

The challenge was urgently to get enough of these new P-51Bs to England in time to make a difference. The first Mustang fighter group of three squadrons was operational by December 1943, with more on their way. Eighth Air Force also received a change at the top. Spaatz returned to England to take overall command of all US strategic air forces in England and Italy, while Major-General Jimmy Doolittle took over the Eighth. Doolittle was a young, dynamic and pioneering aviator who immediately gave orders for his fighters no longer to close-escort the bombers but instead actively to seek out all enemy fighters and attack them. On the way home they were ordered to shoot up any enemy airfields they saw too.

Allied air commanders had been planning an all-out round-the-clock assault on the German aircraft industry for some months, but not until the third week of February 1944 were the conditions right: a big enough gap in the weather and enough long-range fighters.

Operation ARGUMENT began on the night of 19 February with Bomber Command hitting assembly plants at Leipzig. The following day it was the turn of the Eighth. Later in the week, the Fifteenth Air Force in Italy also joined the fray as the biggest air battle of the war to date was played out over the skies of Germany.

'Big Week', as it became known, destroyed 70 per cent of the factories targeted, but where it really hurt the Luftwaffe was in the loss of pilots. In February 1944, Germany lost 2,605 aircraft – a devastating number. The battle for air superiority was not over, but the tide had been turned in favour of the Allies.

P-51B Mustangs escorting
B-24 Liberator heavy bombers.

Allied bomber losses during Big Week were 6.6 per cent for Bomber Command and 6 per cent for the Americans, far more manageable figures than had been suffered by the Eighth earlier when flying far into the Reich. It also suggested that flying by night was no less dangerous than flying by day. What's more, the dramatic increase in the sophistication of navigation aids, bombsights and target-marking techniques meant Bomber Command no longer needed to settle purely for massed area bombing. Those days were over, yet Harris remained wedded to the same strategy he had championed on taking over the command back in February 1942.

In early March 1944, the Eighth joined Bomber Command in attacking Berlin, and with some success now the bombers were escorted by ever-greater numbers of long-range fighters. Harris finally ended the so-called Battle of Berlin on the night of 30 March when he sent his bombers to Nuremberg, site of the infamous Nazi rallies of the 1930s. It was a disaster for the Allies. 'Wholesale slaughter,' wrote Flight Lieutenant 'Rusty' Waughman, a Lancaster pilot in 101 Squadron. He reckoned he had seen at least sixteen bombers go down as the RAF planes were mauled by German night-fighters. 'All of us were pretty tired and shaken!' Waughman added in his diary. Bill Byers had also been on the raid, although he had perhaps been saved by engine trouble that forced him to turn for home early.

Nuremberg would prove the costliest mission of the entire war and confirmed what was already crystal clear to all but Harris: that his vision of massed bombing was not going to bring about the sudden wholesale collapse of the Third Reich.

Throughout March and April of 1944, the Allies – and the Americans especially – continued the strategy of POINTBLANK: to grind down the Luftwaffe and win air superiority over much of western Europe. By now the famed 4th Fighter Group was also equipped with Mustangs. Led by Lieutenant-Colonel Don Blakeslee, before America's entry into the war they had originally formed three volunteer squadrons in the RAF. By early 1944, they were one of the most experienced and highly skilled fighter units in the West and, under Blakeslee's tough, confident and aggressive leadership, the 4th soon had a number of rising aces amongst their number. Men such as Don Gentile, John Godfrey and Jimmy Goodson were becoming household names and able to pass on their knowledge to the new pilots arriving fresh from the States.

By contrast, the old guard of Luftwaffe aces was slowly but surely being whittled down in number as desperate German air commanders made them fly on relentlessly. Fighter pilot losses were utterly unsustainable as new pilots were arriving at front-line squadrons with ever-fewer hours in their logbooks, little chance to train further because of fuel shortages and expected to fly inadequate models of Messerschmitt 109s, not an easy aircraft for the inexperienced to master. Losses through accidents now exceeded 50 per cent. Those who did get airborne were facing American pilots with greater skill and experience, flying superior aircraft. The Germans were being slaughtered.

By mid-April, the Allies had finally won control of the skies over western Europe – and in the nick of time for D-Day. General Dwight D. Eisenhower, the Supreme Allied Commander for the invasion, now took formal control of the strategic air forces as D-Day, set for 5 June 1944, drew closer.

P-38 Lightning (top), P-51D Mustang (middle), P-47 Thunderbolt (bottom), and below (left to right) John Godfrey, Don Gentile and Jimmy Goodson.

Many high-level discussions had taken place over how best to use the strategic air forces to support the forthcoming invasion. Spaatz argued strongly for attacking all German fuel supplies, from Ploesti in Romania – the only oilfield available to Nazi Germany – to various depots and synthetic-fuel plants throughout the Reich. Air Chief Marshal Sir Arthur Tedder, the Deputy Supreme Commander, favoured attacking larger railway centres, marshalling yards and depots in support of the work of the Allied tactical air forces now striking bridges, railways and the German communications network.

In the end, both plans were adopted, although Tedder's Transportation Plan had the priority up to the invasion. Harris, meanwhile, was deeply opposed to playing second fiddle to someone else's plan and would have preferred to keep on hitting German cities. There were also concerns that the Transportation Plan, much of which would be targeted at France, would lead to terrible loss of civilian life amongst those they were about to liberate. However, Bomber Command, especially, proved more than up to the task, attacking their targets with success and comparatively little loss of life – and, interestingly, frequently with greater accuracy than their American allies operating by night.

At the same time, Spaatz's Oil Plan was also under way. By the end of May 1944, this was really hurting the Luftwaffe and Germany as a whole, so much so that the Luftwaffe moved a number of flak units from cities to protect synthetic-fuel plants.

Meanwhile, the Germans had started directing V-1 flying bombs to southern England and V-2 rockets were on their way. Their launch sites, despite being very difficult to hit accurately, were now relentlessly targeted too.

On most days, the Allies could now call on around 2,500 heavy bombers to pummel Germany, but the demands on these resources were considerable. D-Day was finally launched, successfully, on 6 June 1944, but throughout the Battle for Normandy, strategic air forces were repeatedly called upon to support operations on the ground with attacks on Caen, Saint-Lô and numerous other targets, including port cities like Le Havre. After Normandy, there were further ground operations to support, such as MARKET GARDEN, the failed Allied airborne attempt to cross the Rhine at Arnhem.

By the end of September, however, Eisenhower had handed back direct control of the Allied strategic air forces, their successful support of the invasion of Europe completed. The question now was how best to use the mass of heavy bombers to quicken the end of the war. So much had changed. The Luftwaffe, though not beaten, was a shadow of its former self. The Allies had thousands of heavy bombers not hundreds. Accuracy, though still not 'precision', was considerably improved.

Spaatz urged a continuation of the Oil Plan, while, predictably, Harris had not wavered from his preference of continuing to hammer German cities. Unquestionably, both strategies were dramatically reducing Germany's ability effectively to continue the war, but although the outcome of the conflict was in no doubt, Hitler and the Nazi regime made it clear they intended to continue fighting to the bitter end.

Although by this stage of the war it was questionable whether daylight bombing was any more precise than that conducted by night, the Americans were certainly more concerned with the morality of deliberately targeting cities, with their large civilian populations, than were the British.

So the bombing continued. Officially, Allied bombing policy was for oil targets to be the priority and transportation the next most important. In reality, Harris was able to pay lip-service to this directive while still targeting city centres, and especially those cities around the Ruhr industrial area. Cologne, Essen, Dortmund, Koblenz – all were wrecked by the weight of bombs. In all, in 1944, British bombers dropped more than 440,000 tons of bombs on Germany. In the entire Blitz back in 1940–41, the Luftwaffe dropped only 18,000 tons on London.

In February, the Russians asked the Allies to bomb Dresden in eastern Germany. A beautiful medieval city, it was none the less an important rail hub for German troops heading to the southern Eastern Front as well as to Italy. There were also some 127 different factories in Dresden involved in war work. These two factors made it an entirely justifiable target.

However, when Bomber Command attacked in two waves with 805 aircraft on the night of 13/14 February 1945, they targeted the medieval centre, not the military barracks to the north or the marshalling yards. The conditions were ideal, with clear skies and a light wind. Very quickly, a firestorm developed and, tragically for the civilian population, Dresden had far from enough air-raid defences. Latest figures suggest more than 19,000 were killed that night, but Josef Goebbels, the Nazi propaganda chief, cynically claimed 120,000 had perished and hailed it as a British atrocity.

The following night, Chemnitz was attacked, and ten days later, so too was Pforzheim, where one in four civilians was killed. Würzburg was 90 per cent destroyed by the RAF in February 1945, to no obvious military advantage.

The strategic bombing of Germany continued to the very end of the war, and Bomber Command continued to prove it could bomb with skilful precision when asked to do so. In April 1945, 617 Squadron, the Dam Busters, hit the newly built Valentine U-boat assembly plant near Bremen. RAF photo reconnaissance had been watching its construction carefully and realized that, while some of the roof was 15 metres thick with concrete, other parts were just 5 feet. The Dam Busters flew over before a single U-boat had been completed, targeting the weaker part of the roof with 10-ton Grand Slam high-explosive bombs. The attack was entirely successful.

Berlin was attacked for the last time on the night of 20 April 1945 and Hitler's home in the Bavarian Alps at Berchtesgaden was smashed a few days later. The Third Reich lay in ruins and, although by the end of April the Red Army was swarming over Berlin, it was mostly bombs dropped by the RAF, and to a lesser extent the Americans, that had reduced it to a broken, post-apocalyptic shell. That so many other German cities lay in shattered ruins was also largely down to Harris's bombing policy. Almost a million tons of bombs had been dropped on Germany during five long years of Bomber Command's air offensive and cost hundreds of thousands of lives. Almost one in two Bomber Command aircrew was killed during the war.

The morality of the Bomber War has been debated ever since, but there is no doubt that the hammering of Germany caused immense material and economic damage and shortened the war. Air power also allowed the Allies to put fewer men into the front line on the ground. Despite the cost, it did unquestionably save Allied lives.

And the moment the Nazis surrendered, the bombing stopped.

Further Reading

GENERAL HISTORIES

James Holland *The War in the West*, Vol. 1: *Germany Ascendant, 1939–1941*

James Holland *The War in the West*, Vol. 2: *The Allies Fight Back, 1941–1943*

James Holland *Dam Busters*

James Holland *Big Week*

Richard Overy *The Bombing War*

Tami Davis Biddle *Rhetoric and Reality in Air Warfare*

MEMOIRS

Heinz Knoke *I Flew for the Führer*

Adolf Galland *The First and the Last*

Bert Stiles *Serenade to the Big Bird*

Robert S. Johnson *Thunderbolt!*

Truman Smith *The Wrong Stuff*